Be the Light

"I Want to be the Light for Others, so They Can Be the Light for Others, and So On"

BY JESSICA L. MARICLE RN,
REIKI MASTER HOLY FIRE

The contents of this work, including, but not limited to, the accuracy of events, people, and places depicted; opinions expressed; permission to use previously published materials included; and any advice given or actions advocated are solely the responsibility of the author, who assumes all liability for said work and indemnifies the publisher against any claims stemming from publication of the work.

All Rights Reserved
Copyright © 2020 by Jessica L. Maricle RN, Reiki Master Holy Fire

No part of this book may be reproduced or transmitted, downloaded, distributed, reverse engineered, or stored in or introduced into any information storage and retrieval system, in any form or by any means, including photocopying and recording, whether electronic or mechanical, now known or hereinafter invented without permission in writing from the publisher.

Dorrance Publishing Co
585 Alpha Drive
Pittsburgh, PA 15238
Visit our website at *www.dorrancebookstore.com*

ISBN: 978-1-6480-4136-5
eISBN: 978-1-6470-2594-6

Be the Light

"I Want to be the Light for Others,
so They Can Be the Light for Others, and So On"

Table of Contents:

Inspiration for Others vii
Acknowledgments ix
Preface xi

Chapters

Chapter 1: The Accident 1
Chapter 2: The Reality Sets In 5
Chapter 3: The Search for Natural Relief. 7
Chapter 4: God, I Surrender 11
Chapter 5: Taking a Look Back 13
Chapter 6: Meeting Hope 17
Chapter 7: Learning a New Realm 21
Chapter 8: Reiki Becoming a Reality 29
Chapter 9: Not in Kansas Anymore 33
Chapter 10: Newfound Gifts. 39
Chapter 11: Big Dreams 41
Chapter 12: Reiki Master Achieved. 45
Chapter 13: Geographic "Fix" Fails 49
Chapter 14: Home to Reality 55
Chapter 15: Something Finally Clicked 57
Chapter 16: New Perspectives. 59
Chapter 17: Realizations and Validation 61
Chapter 18: Making a Difference 63

I want to be the light for others,
so they can be the light for others and so on.

— JESSICA MARICLE

Acknowledgments

I hope I do my list of acknowledgments justice. I am going to list in no particular order of importance, just relevance.

Cover design and author picture by: Jenna Ann. Thank you for your love and support. My hopes and dreams for you are that you see the beauty in yourself as I see in you. I love you.

I want to thank my husband, kids, and family for supporting me and not locking me up in the loony bin when I started this spiritual and recovery journey. We all know I would rock a strait jacket, but thank you for not making that a reality. Your love and support have meant the world to me. I love you all so very much. Thank you from the bottom of my heart.

Thank you to all my wonderful therapists at Alice Fadden and Associates, my family primary care physician, Dr. Elkins, and Concussion Specialist Angela Rodner. You all were an important part of my healing. Thank you for allowing that to happen and supporting me every step of the way. Even though each step was kicking and screaming. It's very easy to label or judge people, and I appreciate you seeing me as first and foremost a perfectly imperfect human, but human nonetheless and treating me as such.

Thank you to Chris Ellis for showing me passion for life and the importance of driving fast and taking risks. You were truly an amazing soul. Your spirituality and faith in God were inspirational to not only me, but all who knew you. Even after your death, you continue to be a beacon of light for so many, myself included.

Thank you to my many friends far and near for loving me for me even when I didn't love myself. Thank you for not giving up on me and showing me other sides of love, peace, and happiness.

Thank you to all the amazing Reiki folks for showing me a whole new realm and supporting me in my purpose. Thank you, Sharyn Madison, for supporting me in such a loving and supportive way that only a true healer possesses. You are truly an Earth angel, and I hope you know how much I appreciate you.

Thank you, God, my many angels, and spirit guides. I know you truly love me and are supporting me on this crazy journey called life. Even though I am not super natural and can't see or speak to you, I know you are with me. Wayne Dyer said it best when he said, "If you knew who walked beside you at all times on this path that you have chosen, you could never experience fear or doubt again."

Such a beautiful quote.

Thank you, the reader, for taking the time to share in my experience. My intent is it will help another lost soul.

Thank you, to me…

for loving myself…finally!

Preface

I first want to introduce myself, as I am told that is what a preface is for. As you can tell by this statement, I have never been nor did I ever dream of writing a book. But here I am trying to relay all that has happened in the past 18 months, in hopes that it will help someone else.

A bit of background on myself. I come from a small hometown. My graduating high school class was 28 kids. Yes, you just read that right, 28 kids. We don't have a stop light or a gas station in our town. We do have two bars, so that's impressive. Our traffic jams are either cows, deer, turkeys, or other various wildlife and tractors. In fact, just today, I was stopped by two horses in the road. Our area is full of beautiful landscapes with mountains and breathtaking sunsets. Our main street is quaint and charming in its own way. When you attend school events, you typically see at least a couple dozen people that you went to school with. Everyone pretty much knows everyone, which can both be a blessing and a curse.

I was an RN case manager for a home care agency in the area. I loved my job and couldn't imagine doing anything else, and why would I? I had been an RN for over 20 years. I had worked with amazing physicians throughout the years as well as co-workers. I've worked with hematology/oncology, orthopedics, med-surg, geriatrics, finally settling into my calling of home care. My job as a home care case manager was to coordinate care needed for each patient. The unique part was it was in their home, their environment.

I loved working with families and patients in their environment, taking as much time as I needed to teach and make a difference in their everyday life. Home care did not have as much of the corporate bullshit telling me how I was allowed to practice nursing. My office was my home. With its minimal micro-managing, long charting hours, but freedom to care the way I felt patients deserved to be treated, I thought I had everything figured out. I thought I had found my purpose in life. I was wrong, but only partially.

In July of 2018, I was in a car accident that changed my life. I went from having what I thought was everything, to having everything I held in high regards taken away in the blink of an eye.

I not only had to deal with the physical issues from my injuries but mental ones as well. I battle chronic pain, depression, anxiety, and PTSD. All of which roll up into a big ball of fun, fun, go away.

I am sharing my story because I feel that others may have had similar experiences. In my journey at times, I felt overwhelmed, overjoyed, alone, loved, angry, forgiving, confused, enlightened, hopeless, hopeful, depressed, happy… The roller coaster of feelings was endless. I was basically a walking contradiction with an ever-changing mood pattern. I haven't even hit menopause yet; that should be interesting!

My issues were not visible to the naked eye. I looked "normal," talked "normal," walked "normal," smiled for the world to see, but inside I was dying. I was a master of disguise, and my disguise was being happy. I don't believe I ever had that as a goal in my life:

"I think I will fake being happy for the world to be more comfortable around me."

In my journey to recovery, I am finding something more, myself, being authentic to my true self, my spiritual side, and my real purpose. It's a continuous journey that, honestly, I hope never ends. Truth be told, I am not even close to fully understanding. I would love to tell you I have it all figured out, but that is just not the case. I have learned along the way, laughed, cried, screamed, cursed like a drunken sailor, and for the first time ever understood why people commit suicide. That last diddy is not something I am proud of, but awareness is key.

> The loss I had felt brought me to my knees.
> From kneeling, I prayed and started to rise.

Chapter 1
The Accident

July 18, 2018, started like any other day. I woke to a bright sunny day, birds chirping as usual. The coffee was filling the house with its heavenly aroma, welcoming me after a night's slumber. I showered, allowing the warm water to wash away my cares and worries for the upcoming day.

I sat at my computer, receiving my patients' information from corporate and reviewing their charts. I reviewed orders, read over disciplines notes, and planned my day accordingly. The beauty of being a home care case manager was that my office was mainly at home with the occasional visit to the cooperate office. I called and confirmed all my visits. This was pretty much my daily routine. This morning was no different, or so I thought.

The initial drive seemed normal, uneventful even. I, however, missed my turn to my first patient's house. Apparently, my brain was on auto pilot to his old home as he recently moved. This simple mistake turned into my nightmare. I noticed a turnaround, slowed, put my blinker on, and proceeded with my left turn…and this is when my life changed forever.

The woman behind me was apparently not paying attention to my blinker, brake lights, or my intent to turn, and passed me crossing a double yellow line, hitting me at 55 mph. The full impact was directly to my driver's door, totaling my car with me in direct contact. I am still unsure what possessed her to pass me on the left side. She never hit her brakes; no skid marks, no attempt to stop. It was full speed ahead.

It happened so fast! The crashing sound, air bags being deployed, the first impact of her car, then the second impact as my car was being catapulted off her car into the guard rail. My initial response honestly was, *Holy shit, I was in an accident!* I felt blessed that I was alive! I felt for blood, none—phew. My glasses were sideways on my head but intact. My lips were numb, but the initial assessment was, *Okay, I'm alive.* I called 911 as soon as I was done with my mini assessment and gained enough sense. I was trying to relay to the operator what happened. I can recall the panic in my voice and in every ounce of my body like it was yesterday. The operator then asked if others were involved.

My thoughts then turned to the other driver: *Oh my God, how is the other driver?* I couldn't see anything but airbags. I couldn't see anyone walking around, and I couldn't get out of my car. My door was completely demolished. My panic worsened, and the nurse was kicking in as I was trying to get out of my car to make sure the other driver was okay. I wasn't sure if the person was badly injured, a family member, friend, or if children were involved…or worse, if someone was dead. I could not process in my head how to get out of my car. At that moment, I was pinned.

A man came to the window and asked if I was okay.

"I'm alive, but what about the other driver?" I asked almost screaming at him, "What about the other driver, are they okay?"

The man told me, "She is okay, she's out of her car and walking around."

He then asked me what happened, and I told him I was trying to turn left, and she passed me, then wham!

The next moments were a blur. I called my husband to tell him about the accident. I could hear the concern in his voice as he told me he would be right there and that he loved me. After the man left my window, the police arrived, the ambulance and my husband. I am still not sure how my husband made it in the same amount of time as the ambulance, but he did nevertheless. I could see the panic and sure relief as he saw that I was alive. At this point, a police officer assisted me out of the car through the passenger side of the car. My knees were trembling, and again I was just so thankful to be alive. My husband hugged me with such pure love and gratitude, his chest was my safe spot.

There were multiple police at this time, the fire department, and an ambulance. As I looked around, I was in disbelief about what happened. I saw my kids running down the road, yelling, "Mom!" I could see the fear and relief in their eyes when they saw me. We all hugged and I told everyone I was okay to console them, but inside I was terrified.

Assessing my car and the damage, I realized the outcome could have been totally different. I believe God and my angels were with me that day. I was a fireman in my younger years on an extrication team. I knew all too well that side impacts were deadly. Things inside your body move and tear away, that have no business moving. I have had to do numerous extrications for body removals. This was not a typical accident to walk away from. I was feeling very blessed that my family was not having to plan my funeral.

The time came when the other driver started to walk towards me, my concern was for her. I asked her, "Are you okay?" and the most unexpected thing happened.

She SCREAMED at me, "NO, I AM NOT OKAY! DO I LOOK OK? YOU CAME OUT OF NOWHERE!" as she continued to walk and climb into the ambulance. I honestly was baffled. I couldn't believe that not only did she think I appeared out of thin air, but had no concern whatsoever for my safety.

I looked at my husband and had to ask, "Did she seriously just say that?" So not only was it a bright sunny day not a cloud in the sky, but there was approximately a football field of visibility! How in the hell did she think I just "came out of nowhere"? This response later in my journey became pure anger and hatred that I had to overcome.

The police officer must have seen the sheer bewilderment of what just took place. He reassured me that it would be okay and continued to assess my well-being. The other driver had climbed into the ambulance. I knew I needed to be assessed in the ER, so I had my husband take me.

At the emergency room, the shock was setting in and the adrenaline was doing some crazy things to my body. I felt so nauseated, the pain started to set in, the numbness in my lips. I was put on a board with neck stabilization until the CT scan was cleared. Scans and x-rays ruled out any fractures or immediate threats. I thought I was in the clear. We were told that I most likely will be "very sore," had a concussion, and to get rest! Okay, easy enough! Wow, I was lucky.

Recovery will be a walk in the park, rest, return to work, easy, I thought, and I thought wrong.

Chapter 2
The Reality Sets In

The aftermath of what happened started to set in. My injuries included head, left shoulder, neck, and lower back. I noticed that my thoughts were scrambled as well as my words. I was thinking one thing and would say something completely off the wall. My daughter would get a chuckle of course as I asked her to get me a "turkey" when I meant "tomato," or when I asked her to load the napkins in the dishwasher. We can laugh now, but at the time, it was so frustrating as well as embarrassing. Here I was, a pretty educated woman, articulate most of the times, and now, I sounded like I was just learning to talk. Perhaps I was injured more than was first diagnosed.

Our search began for a new car, and I couldn't focus on details of the car, prices, options, nothing. My brain was in this perpetual fog. This was very uncharacteristic for me. With my personality and my profession as a case manager, I was never like this. I could overthink a bowel movement. My mind was always going 1,000 miles an hour, thinking and analyzing everything. The details of buying a car was like I was suddenly thrown into learning to be an astronaut in another language. The information would come at me, and I was a deer in the head lights. I couldn't process anything. I figured I was still in shock. Or perhaps there was something more going on.

I went to my primary physician and told her what I was experiencing, and she told me that I had a concussion and that sometimes the affects can be the same as a stroke. Well that certainly made sense. Now mind you I have been an RN for 20-plus years and at that moment could not tell you the effects of a concussion! My brain decided to take a vacation without the rest of me. Lord knows at that very moment, I needed a vacation; I just wish my brain would have clued my body into its departure.

The pain and soreness at this point had started to set in as well. I figured it would get better and was told to rest and that's exactly what I did. One week later, I returned to my doctor, and the symptoms were still not improving. The pain continued, and my mind was still on vacation in some far-off, distant land. I again was told to rest and that it may take time to resolve, relaying that my brain and body were severely bruised.

I was referred to physical therapy. I was pretty apprehensive, as I was still under the illusion that with rest, I would be back to normal. My therapy started, and I quickly realized that my injuries were worse than I thought. Everything is connected in the back, neck, and shoulder region. Each time I did exercises for one part, it triggered another part of my body. For the next six months, I went to therapy three to four days a week concentrating on stretching and trying to get the muscles to relax. They were in a constant spasm, and the pain continued. From the concussion, I still had brain fog, word finding issues, as well as daily headaches, all of which worsened with the spasms in my neck and shoulder which then triggered migraines. Up until this point, I very rarely had headaches and had never had a migraine in my life! Now it was an every day occurrence, as common as waking up and breathing.

Referral after referral, doctor after doctor, appointments, more referrals, more therapy, eventual surgery to the shoulder for torn rotator cuff and impaired mobility. My life consisted at this point of waking, appointment after appointment and going to bed. Not actually sleeping, however that would be preposterous! I kept thinking things were going to get better. I was wrong. They kept getting worse!

Chapter 3
The Search for Natural Relief

December 24, as I was Christmas shopping, my phone rang. It was my employer. I was told that I was about to lose my job unless I could return by January. My career was now on the line! My benefits, my retirement, pension, my "plan" were now on the brink of being destroyed. My career was officially altered. January came and went, and so did my dream job.

After about six months of referrals, scans, MRIs, I was told that I needed surgery. My shoulder was not improving, and the pain from the shoulder was making it difficult to make any progress with therapy because we could not separate any of the body parts. I had my surgery in March of 2019. I was hopeful that this was the answer: "Okay, fix the shoulder, the spasms will stop in the shoulder neck region, and my headaches will go away!"

Nope! My shoulder pain eventually improved. The spasms, however, did not, so the headaches continued daily! God, please make this go away!

I was referred to a pain clinic. The options presented to me seemed viable. Injections to stop the spasms, which in turn would stop compressing the herniated discs in my neck and back, which were triggering more spasms. Okay, made sense to me. I was poked and prodded like a voodoo doll. I had a cervical injection, trigger point injections, spinal facet injections, as well as SI injections. None of which worked and hurt like hell. The facet injection I was told "it's not that bad," but in reality, it was the worst of them all. The pain was so excruciating that I was white knuckling the corner of the table I was on. Being told over and over, "hold still, we are almost done," I cried to the point of hyperventilating, my lips became numb, the room was spinning, and the nausea was overpowering. I can honestly say I would not have felt bad for puking on the doctor that day. I was infuriated afterwards and told the doctor as well as the nurse that there was no reasonable explanation to put me through that much pain. I had some very colorful language; let me tell you, the "F" word flew very fluently out of my mouth that day! This is what healthcare has become? No compassion whatsoever. I was disgusted to say the least!

The injections didn't work; pain medications made me sick; Prednisone caused a stomach ulcer, as well as Ibuprofen. So now not only was the pain poorly controlled, let's add a bit of flame to my stomach. Even water caused my stomach to burn like I swallowed a blow torch. I was limited on what I could take.

I wanted more natural ways to control my pain. I was quickly realizing the faults of "modern medicine" as this pill or that pill was the "fix all," and they all made me sick. The pain clinic seemed only interested in poking me or pumping me full of medicine and injections. In fact, when I told them I wanted more natural solutions to pain, I was told they could no longer assist me, but to come back in three months. Why? So the insurance company can pay you to do nothing? By this point, my view on the medical world was changing quickly. As a patient, I was realizing that insurance dictated everything, more so than even I thought. I was just a chart number to some or an insurance claim away from being paid. I was ushered in like cattle. At times being treated like I was "just making it up." This medical world that I loved for so long was letting me down. What happened to compassion? What happened to talking and listening to our patients? What happened to the doctor knows best, not the insurance company? Hell, half the time, it's not even the doctor you see. What happened to taking our patients' word on pain and not judging them? These were all core values I learned in nursing school.

I was referred to a Concussion Clinic and was diagnosed with PTSD as well as depression and anxiety disorder. Man the "good" news just wouldn't stop. It was about this time that it really started to sink in that my injuries were not just temporary. Not only physically but emotionally as well. Every time I looked at my car, "Yup, I got that because of my accident." Each doctor appointment, "Yup, I have all these appointments because of my accident." Everything I did reminded me of my accident. The anxiety of it all was over powering. Over the next six months, my mood as well as my outlook was less than stellar. After a year, the depression had spiraled out of control, and I needed to ask for help. For me, being a caregiver for so long, to ask for help made me feel very weak and extremely vulnerable. I went from being a person that people looked to for help to the person asking. Even small tasks, I had to ask for help like at the grocery store, doing chores, lifting heavy objects, the list is endless. Prior to this, my husband and I built our own home with our bare hands! I skied, I would do landscaping, digging and planting for hours, mountain biked, could lift a 50 lb. bag of feed and throw a bale of hay like a man. I had been told by numerous people on various occasions that I worked harder than most "men I know." To me, that was a huge compliment, and I took great pride in working hard. My husband and I would ride on the motorcycle for hours, "just because." Now I needed help with groceries!

I was put on an antidepressant as well as a sleeping pill. This regimen then triggered more nightmares, and the "fun" continued. I at one point envisioned the barrel of a gun in my mouth and could for the first time in my life understand why people committed suicide. Prior to this moment, I felt people were quitters or were weak. Well...I was weak and so vulnerable. I was tired of the pain and the loss I felt was so overwhelming that suicide was tantalizing and actually seemed like a good option. This was my breaking point. Thankfully, although I did not love myself at this point, my love for my family was greater than the pain or loss I felt. For them, I asked for help.

Chapter 4
God, I Surrender

I remember the day well. At my lowest point, walking up the sidewalk to my doctor. It was cold outside, drizzly, wet, and a snowy miserable kind of day. I would have rather crawled in a hole than face my demons. Love is a powerful thing, and it's the only thing that made me take one step in front of the other. I waited patiently to see my doctor, trying so hard to keep it together and not cry. My hands were sweaty, and I was in a panic. I just wanted to run away from it all and pretend it was just a dream. Finally, the time came, and I heard a soft knock at the door.

"Is it okay to come in?"

"Yes" came out of my mouth, when I just wanted to say, "no go away!"

In she came bringing in a student and a Nurse Practitioner trainee along with her…perfect! Now not only do I have to ask for help from my Doctor, I get to be the training subject for others. On any other day, this would have never bothered me, but this particular day I felt exposed for the world to see. She asked if they could stay, I was too weak to say no.

She asked in her sweet voice with her smile, "So how have you been?"

That was all it took; I started sobbing and pleading with my doctor. I felt so weak, so helpless, and unbelievably hopeless. I could not contain the sorrow I felt. I think if I could have gotten on my knees and begged, I would have. I sobbed uncontrollably instead, shoulders jerking, tears flowing and crying for help.

"I can't do this by myself anymore, please help me!"

I couldn't stand the overwhelming anger, pain, the feeling of loss any more. The physical pain on this particular day was unbearable, which intensified the emotional pain I felt. My head was in a vise; my body ached and screamed for relief. She had to give me an injection to break the pain cycle. Some of the physical pain subsided; however, the emotional pain was still so strong.

I had always been such a positive person, looking at the brightness and lessons in each event that happened in my life. I at one point even "thanked" my new car. "If my old car did not save my life, I would not have a new car," thinking that if I changed my perspective, then my emotional health would improve. I had always taken the stand that everything happens for a reason. I struggled to find the reason in any of this. I struggled with just being alive.

Depression was something that I had only witnessed thus far. I never actually got the full concept of it until then. I was told, "Oh, it's not that bad, focus on the good," or "I'm in pain, too, I still go to work," or "It's all in your head." Umm, yeah, no shit, literally the headaches are ridiculous! These comments I know were supposed to make me feel better, but in reality, made things worse. I questioned my self-worth! If they can do it, why can't I? I should be able to just snap my fingers and poof, I'm not depressed or in pain anymore. I never understood, nor do the people who have never suffered with depression or pain. It is invisible, and people with depression can hide it extremely well. We are masterminds of illusion. I learned to smile and say, "I'm fine," and make people believe I had nothing wrong. I was learning to be a PRO! In fact, with my theatrical performance, I think I could have won a Grammy. In the process, though, I was becoming anti-social because, let's face it: being fake is exhausting. Being in pain is depressing, and being depressed is depressing! Pain, depression, more spasms, more pain, more depression, no sleep, more depression, more exhaustion, more pain, more depression—holy shit, get me off of this fucking roller coaster! Spiraling out of control. Not knowing what to do, think, or feel. I finally just fell to the ground, and could not get back up. There was no light in my world. It was complete darkness. I was on the ground in a fetal position on the cold, damp ground. It didn't matter who was around, or who cared or loved me. It was so dark I couldn't see, hear or feel anything. No light…I was alone.

Okay…God, I surrender! I give in. Please help me, show me the way, guide me with your light. I can't do this by myself anymore! I prayed; that was all I could do, pray.

Chapter 5
Taking a Look Back

As I said in my preface, I had physical, mental, and spiritual realizations. Now we back track to the start of my spiritual awakening if you will.

I have had many experiences in my life to question my spirituality. For example, when I was 18, my mother was very sick with cancer. One week prior to her passing, she told me that "Nana came to visit me." My Nana had passed away years prior. Although I just assumed it was her pain medication talking, I did ask, "What did she say?"

She replied, "It's not time yet, Annie."

One day prior to my mom passing, I was exhausted and decided to go back to my apartment. It was daytime, midafternoon. I fell asleep, but as quickly as I fell asleep, I woke sitting straight up in bed. I said to my friend, Rachel, at the time, "Who is the man standing in the hallway?"

Confused, she looked and said, "There is no one standing in the hallway."

I replied, "Yes, there is, he is right there."

I pointed down the hallway at the man. Looking again at Rachel then back to the hallway, this time, he was gone. The man I saw was a Jesus figure. He had a white robe, a glow to him. He had a beard but not super long and shoulder length hair. I can still see him in my mind as I did back then, 28 years ago, his image was that clear. I wasn't afraid of him; if anything, I felt more at peace. I believe he came to tell me that everything was going to be okay. Shortly after this, my mom had passed away. That evening my brother, grandmother, and myself each had a weird experience. My brother heard what he thought was the TV, but checked each room, and there was no TV on, but he had heard voices. My grandmother heard music; same thing, no radio on, but she heard the music. I was at my home, petting and loving on my cat as he had apparently missed me dearly. He was purring and rubbing lovingly against me, then all of the sudden, he started to run around the room. He was jumping around hissing and growling like he was trying to get away from something. Then he stopped as quickly as he started. I believe it was my mom saying goodbye. I think she could have done it without scaring the shit out of my poor cat. None the less, it was a nice moment.

When I worked with Oncology patients, I had held the hands of more dying patients than I could count, and they all had one thing in common. They all saw and started to talk to relatives who had passed prior to them. In fact, when this would happen, we knew the time was getting near for them to pass. Typically, this is when we started to call in the family and tell them time was near. This is a common occurrence with most medical professionals, all of us sharing similar stories.

Recently, my dear friend Rita's husband was about to pass. Something in me asked, "Have you been seeing angels?"

She looked at me curiously and said, "Yes, since before Christmas."

She proceeded to tell me that she could not make out faces but could see a smokey image around her husband's bed. She said she has not told anyone because she didn't want them to think she was crazy. I told her that I believed her. She then lovingly started to talk about her best friend growing up and all the people who had already passed. Showing me and talking about pictures she had in her room. Her and her best friend were in choir together and played piano.

I asked Rita, "Have you been hearing music, too?"

She said, "Yes, how do you know this stuff?" I explained what I had learned over the years with the people that have passed. I told her I believed her best friend was with her, and this was why she was hearing music and seeing the smokey images. She was warmed by the image of their friends and family coming to take him home. Two days later, her husband of 76 years passed.

My belief at this point was that I felt spirits were real. I believed in a higher power. I didn't, however, dive into the spirit guides, souls, purpose in life, or any other belief other than, yup, dead relatives come to greet you when you die. I guess my belief system at this point was pretty basic.

One year prior to my accident, I was visiting with one of my patients. I entered his home, and we greeted each other as usual.

I said, "Hello my friend, how are you doing today?"

He told me of a new pain he had in his foot. I quizzed him as a good nurse would do to find the source of his pain.

"Any injury? Redness, swelling, new shoes, fall, twist?"

To all of which, he replied, "No, nothing! I just woke up this morning, and it hurt!"

"Okay," I replied. "Let me look at it."

As I was assessing the color and size of his foot, I touched his ankle, working my hand down his foot to the tip of his toes. In my head, answering my questions, no swelling, temperature was good, good strong pulse, good color, and so on. He then looked at me with a puzzled look on his face and said very matter of fact, "What did you just do?"

I was equally puzzled and said, "What do you mean?"

He continued to tell me that his pain was completely gone!

"Umm, well you got me, all I did was touch your foot." We both just looked at each other, and I giggled, saying, "SWEET! The pain's gone!" laughing it off.

His wife, overhearing what was taking place, asked, "Do you have Reiki?"

Well, I had no clue what in hell that was! I replied, "Who-key?"

She proceeded to tell me it was energy healing with the hands. At this point in my life, I was pretty much a typical "medical person" who believed in the power of medicine, not energy work. I asked her questions, but in the back of my mind honestly thought, *Wow she really needs to get more sleep!*

She then asked, "Has anything like this had happened before?" It didn't take long for me to think of a few more occasions that pain had just "gone away" with my touch, but I just thought it was a coincidence. She then told me, "There are no coincidences."

Well, maybe not, but I thought if I seriously had power shooting out of my hands to magically heal people, then I'd have a line a mile long, and I'd be rich beyond belief healing people.

Actually, what a cool image…healing people with touch! That would actually be pretty amazing!

Reality in my mind set in, and although it was a nice thought, it was a bit on the crazy side. My medical portion of my brain would not allow me to accept this belief at that time.

I replied, "No, I'm just a nurse," and left it at that.

Chapter 6
Meeting Hope

About three months prior to my accident, my husband was working on a job, and I decided to stop to bring him a candy bar and soda. The home belonged to friends of a friend who was asked to remodel the home. My husband was brought in to do some dry wall. The woman of the house was a beautiful woman named Hope and her husband's name was Mike.

Hope had battled ovarian cancer and at that point was in remission. She was such an inspiration and was so full of life. From our first conversation we talked openly like we had known each other our whole lives. She was so kind, gentle, funny, smart, and very spiritual. I loved her zest for life and the sparkle in her eyes when she talked about her adventures. She loved to travel and told me how much she had loved Maine and the ocean. My husband and I had planned a trip to Maine, and she told me all the hot spots to hit and see while there. She gave me a beautiful picture of a lighthouse there and said, "You have to see this while you are there…it is amazing."

We had a lovely visit, but life took over, and we did not see each other again for a while.

Months later, after my accident, I noticed on social media that she was traveling by motorcycle to all these absolutely incredible places. I anxiously followed her posts, seeing her dream of travel come to life. The pictures were of beautiful mountains, water falls, sunsets, the ocean, and ziplining!

Her eyes, however, told a different story, and I knew in my gut this was her last ride. I didn't realize at this time that "reading people" was a gift; I thought it was just being observant. But her, I could read like a book.

I reached out to her when she returned and said, "Okay, what's really going on?" and she proceeded to tell me that her cancer was back, and there was no hope for cure or remission this time. Her hospice nurse was coming that Friday. My heart sank, and I offered my friendship as best as I could. I visited with Hope often. We talked and giggled and told each other stories of our lives, and she quickly became someone that I greatly admired. Hope was not only extremely spiritual, but she had a way of understanding the soul like no one I had ever met. She was also one of the most free-spirited, wild ladies I have ever met.

One day in particular, she asked if we could drive to the lake as she wanted to take her pride mustang out for a ride.

"Umm, hell yeah, that sounds amazing!"

Her mustang was a beautiful baby blue color and was fast as hell! We left her driveway, and she put it sideways in the road, squealing and bellowing smoke from the tires. She lit up like a Christmas tree, yelling, "YAH BABY!"

I on the other hand thought I had shit my pants a little. I'm pretty sure my facial expression was priceless. All I could picture was and image of myself on a roller coaster with hair standing straight up, screaming my fool head off, with a death grip on the bar holding me in! It was both terrifying and exhilarating at the same time. She, of course, laughed hysterically at my reaction then cranked the radio and sang along to the music. I was a bit more reserved than her; well, actually, she was way wilder than my more cautious self. I think that's why we meshed so well.

The day was a perfect fall day; the weather was beautiful. The lake was just as calm as could be, like glass. When we got there, she parked, and a meter reader was there and kindly gave us free parking.

"Sweet!" She told me that God always provides! We talked a lot of our past, trials, and tribulations. We actually had quite a bit in common. I was sad to think that such a beautiful soul had been through so much grief in her life. How she maintained such a positive attitude was honestly just remarkable.

She saw the beauty in every situation, even some of the darkest situations. I didn't know how she stayed so strong. Even her cancer was a blessing! She told me that she would have never met so many wonderful people had she not had it. Wow, I don't think I have ever heard anyone say that cancer was a blessing. She saw blessings in everything. She would tell me it's all about perspective. And she was right! Any situation can be looked at one of two ways, good or bad. Kind of like the number 6. If you look at it one way, it's a 6 but if you turn it over, it's a 9. Same squiggly line, but different meaning and different perspective.

A butterfly had flown by, and she said, "Hi Diane" then proceeded to tell me of a woman that she went to chemotherapy with. Diane also had ovarian cancer, and they both had formed a special bond. Diane was a big part of Hope's life during her chemo. Diane's family becoming Hope's family. They were inseparable; there for each other every step of the way. Diane, unfortunately, had passed away, and Hope was devastated at the loss. She told me that Diane always said she would return as a butterfly. So, from then on, every time she saw a butterfly, she knew it was Diane coming to say hi and check on her dear friend. What a beautiful way to remember her friend. Now I can't help but think of Hope every time I see a butterfly fly by.

On our way back to the car, she asked if I could drive, as she was pretty exhausted from the day. On our way home, we stopped at an overlook and admired the amazing view of the lake and mountains surrounding it. It was very surreal. She told me to enjoy every moment and to always look for the blessings. Saying that the blessings were bountiful. I just need to recognize them. They could be large or small. Simple, like a smile or nice gesture. She continued to say that God will always provide. Maybe not the way I think he should, but I will always have what I need. I just have to maintain the faith. Then, we returned to the car and continued back home. When we got fairly close to her house, she instructed me to "slow down"; the speed limit was actually going up so I was confused. I did as she said, and all of the sudden, she yelled, "Now PUNCH it, Punch that bitch to the floor!" I did as she asked, and I was the one lighting up like a Christmas tree. Holy shit, that car could move; the exhilaration was awesome!

I yelled, "So this is what it feels like to get a Hard on!"

She laughed hysterically and told just about everyone we knew about that. Seeing such joy in her eyes as she told the story brought me happiness and such a beautiful memory of my friend. We were both kids in a candy store that day, barely able to contain our excitement.

Another day, we were talking, and she had told me that when she was going through her chemotherapy that she had received Reiki. Huh, okay, this is the second time that I have heard this term. I asked her if it worked, and she assured me that, "Oh, yes, it was wonderful!"

I picked her brain about this magical treatment, how it felt, who, what, why, where?

She asked me, "Why so many questions?" and I began to tell her my story about the patient and how I touched his foot and his pain went away.

She smiled at me and said, "The first time I met you, I knew you were different."

I took that as a huge compliment. She went on to tell me that I have this positive energy about me. She also told me that she felt I did have this gift and that maybe the accident "was no accident, maybe it was God's way of telling you that you need to do something different." Well, I can honestly say I hadn't looked at the accident in any positive way whatsoever!

I began to question my life, my purpose, my very being. What if the accident was "no accident"? What if it was God's way of knocking me on my ass to listen to him? Apparently, I needed a good knock in the head. Things started to turn, my thoughts, questions, even my perspectives started to change.

Chapter 7
Learning A New Realm

My life was taking crazy turns from the accident to meeting and talking with Hope, and my recovery or lack thereof. Our spiritual conversations were so fascinating. She opened my mind to a whole new realm of possibilities. I felt like I needed help and guidance on a new level, a spiritual one. This was very unfamiliar territory to me.

We went to church when I was a kid. My dad would drag me kicking and screaming; man did I hate going! But I always felt better afterwards, that I do remember. I never considered myself to be religious. We went to multiple different churches depending on who my dad liked as a pastor. So, if anything I considered myself to be a religious mutt. I guess maybe this was a good thing, as I never really was obsessed with one versus another. I believed in a higher power I call God but respect if others call it by different names. I believe in Jesus, heaven, and angels. I do not believe in organized religion because in my mind it separates us, and I believe we are all ONE. My God is no better than yours. I think really, if anything, each "religion" per say are very similar. It's called or looked at differently depending on region or how you grew up. No different than me calling my grandmother "Gram" and others calling her "Nana," "Grammy," "Grandma," "MeeMee," "Naunie," "Mamasita," or "Nama Duck" (which is what I am lovingly called).

I decided to go to the psychic I had gone to years prior. I felt the need for her guidance. What I learned from her that day was a life changing experience. First, she told me that a man in green entered the room and told me that he was "there for the duration." He "connected to me through healing." She was able to describe him in great length. "He has brown wavy hair, parted to the side, green 3/4 sleeves, his hair was wavy like 'Meat Head' in *All in the Family*. He placed his hands on me, stating 'Bless my daughter.' My father was still alive, so this puzzled me. None of the men in my family who have passed fit this description. I was baffled on who this might be.

She then continued with telling me that another man entered and was "bowing to you, very sarcastically." She laughed and very theatrically bowed, "I bowwwww to you," then stated, "but there is gratitude as well." She proceeded to tell me that this man was holding what appeared to be crutches up, stating, "Look, I don't need these anymore!" Then relayed that I helped him with his legs. I knew immediately who this was. It was a young man who I had taken care of for many years tending to wounds on his legs. He passed away a few months prior. He at different times in the reading was seen skate boarding, swimming, or just running and having fun. I was very fond of him. We had a very special relationship. His death was a great loss for me. These images made me so happy because he had been in a wheelchair his whole life. It still gives me such joy to think of him this way. He then said "You took care of me, and now I get to take care of YOUUUU," pointing at me laughing and being very theatrical. Then stated, "Okay, sis," as he left.

Next my mother and grandmother came into the room bantering back and forth about who the mother was, "No, I'm the mother, no, I'm the mother, No I am...how about you?" as they both pointed to me. My mother had passed away when I was 18, and my grandmother took on the mother role. This scenario sounded just like them. She proceeded and said they were joined in and united in paradise. This made me happy as they fought terrible in waking life. My grandmother then stepped forward presenting me with two baskets. Both wicker with one large handle each. One with herbs and "the other, oh, that's just the red berries" My grandmother was very assertive about the basket with the herbs, putting if forward for special attention. Stating, "They are medicinal," and said I should study natural forms of healing. The other basket she wanted me to know about, as it was important, but to focus more on the herbal basket. At this point, the man in green agreed with my grandmother to study natural forms of healing. Again reinforcing that he was connected to me in healing and would help me.

Later in the reading, my mother was very pensive in thought, sitting at a desk writing and signing an important "book or legal document," something that my brother and I would both read. She was deep in thought and said, "Read it with fondness as I have done," proceeding to tell me that "your dad will speak more of me," but again to look at the papers with fondness. I was confused and did not understand what this meant. Later in the year, I had discovered that she was referring to her Last Will and Testament after a discussion my father and I had regarding her will, so this finally made perfect sense.

My first reading I had, a year prior to this one, was very special as it proved that my mom had been with me all along. She had told me of events that my mom had witnessed in my life and reinforced that she was there for all of it. Even in death, my mom was always there for me. This reading was no exception other than my grandmother had joined her since my last reading. It did, however, open up some questions, like who was the man in green, how was he connected to me in healing? What is the Natural Healing I need to pursue?

The day was a whirlwind of information and possibilities. I excitedly told Hope about the reading, and she said, "What about Reiki? That's natural, and what about essential oils and herbs?"

Our conversations were thick into the topics of natural healing and multiple things she had tried. She was a wealth of knowledge with herbs, oils, and Reiki. She included many of the natural healing in her daily life and pain regimen. It was so much information, and honestly, I really had a hard time absorbing it all. My brain was a whirlwind.

Hope's own pain at this point was poorly controlled. I was desperate to help her. I was willing to put my pretenses aside that Reiki was crazy and that I didn't have this ability. I did a lot of research on the topic. I also read two inspirational books by Raven Keyes and decided what the heck. I found a Reiki class that was in Buffalo and was so excited that one was in my home state. I signed up quickly, paid the money, went to put the class in my calendar and realized that we had our son's wedding that weekend. I was so excited about the class that it did not click that it was on that weekend. My heart sank like a sinking ship. I knew I wanted to help Hope. I knew her time was becoming more limited. I continued to look for other classes and found one in Connecticut…ugh. I Map Quested it, realized that it was do-able, but as with Buffalo, I needed help. I spoke with my husband, and he agreed to drive me, as there was no possible way I could drive that far. He requested time off for the trip and was approved. Yeah, it was set, I was going to officially learn how to do Reiki. I can honestly say I was still pretty skeptical of the power of Reiki but was willing to give it a try for my friend. And hey…my dead grandmother had presented me a basket, so it's gotta be real right?

The events just got weirder and weirder to be honest. I really thought I was losing my mind. Hope had told me at one point that numbers were messages from heaven and angels trying to talk to us. In fact, they spoke to us in many different forms. I found this really interesting. So, I started to do research on this. I became a sponge for knowledge. I read books on Reiki, articles on spiritual awakening, numbers, witching hour, and "what they mean." I read one thing, and it would lead to another. Many of the articles I read led to wounded healers and the Law of Attraction or Manifestation. I was extremely overwhelmed, but hopeful at the same time, that maybe I would be able to help my friend.

Hope one day asked me to stop at McDonald's to pick her up a coffee.

I said, "Sure no problem." As usual I was running late and just happened to look at the time while in the drive through, and it was 11:11. I really had no idea what this was or the significance of this spiritual number. After I got the coffee, I decided to look it up. My mind was blown away when it told me it was a very spiritual number, meaning I was awakening to vibratory changes around me, establishing myself in the conscious collective. It's also felt to work with the angelic realm. Some people feel that it is a "star seed" awakening to its purpose and mission on Earth (a star

seed is a human with a soul that did not originate on Earth). At some point, I had also read about Archangel Raphael. He is the patron saint for the sick and the healers, he associates with the color green. This prompted me to look up a picture of him and was blown away. A man in green, 3/4 sleeve robe, brown wavy hair parted to the side. Somewhere in the moment, I also read something about red berries. I honestly felt my heart in my throat. I told Hope about this, and she said, "Yeah, I believe Raphael is with you, he's with all the healers." Wow! She was so calm and matter of fact, "Yup."

I was freaking out. *Okay, relax…it's just a sign from heaven saying that I have an archangel sending me messages. Well shit, sign me up, I'm officially going crazy! I'll take my straitjacket in hot pink please.*

She then proceeded in saying, "And just to show you that he is here for you and he wants you to believe, you will come into some money if you believe…do you believe? If you believe, by the end of the day you will come into some money, maybe by finding it in the washing machine, or a pocket… like $5 or something."

I said that I would believe: "Okay, I believe!"

On my way home that night, I stopped at the gas station. Hmm, well screw it, and I bought a scratch off…I WON $5, so I bought another, and I WON AGAIN…so I bought another, and I WON a third time, winning a Take 5 ticket. I was blown away! Okay, God, you got my attention!

Before my class, I decided that maybe I needed to experience Reiki myself. I had no clue about it, let alone what it felt like. I went to Psychic Fair and, to be fair, felt very out of place. The more people I met though, the more I saw the word Reiki. A majority of the people offering services were trained in Reiki, then proceeded to other modalities of healing. I was blown away by all the information I received on crystal healing, herbs, Karmic healing, acupuncture, biomedical feedback…the list goes on. Good gravy, my mind was completely shook.

While there, I decided on a Reiki treatment. I have to say I really didn't feel much and was pretty disappointed. She did, however, tell me that she envisioned an angel with big wings coming into my heart space, that image in itself was pretty cool. She also saw a beautiful blue butterfly quickly come in and go out. This made me think of Hope's friend Diane.

I then had Aura photography done, and this was pretty cool. She said I was in a big transition in healing and becoming more spiritual. She also cussed the Granddaddy of all cuss words, and I laughed and was ecstatic that I could still be me and still cuss. Somehow along the way of learning about angels, spirit guides, God, Jesus, etc., I thought I had to be holier than thou to be a "true healer." She quickly corrected me and told me I just needed to be me. Let me tell you this was a huge relief! Like the weight of the world just came off my shoulders. I really questioned if I was going to be good enough. Hope told me that God knows we screw up and loves us anyways. This gives me comfort because I sure have made some mistakes in my life.

The day before I left, I felt the need to see a different Reiki practitioner. Her name was Sherry and was a well-known and respected in our local community. I met with her and explained my journey thus far. She listened like she was a kid listening to her favorite story. Sherry was so enthusiastic to hear my tale. She had told me that she believed what I was going through and that she also had very similar instances and realizations in her life. She also told me she felt I was a healer in my previous life, stating she got an image of me working with herbs and berries, which prompted me to tell her about my reading. She then got up and gave me a spiritual drawing from a woman who will get images in her head of different things. She handed me a card with Raphael on it. WOW! I then told her my tale of Reiki, and why I was interested in it. Proceeding to tell her I was going to a class to learn how, she said she felt that I would be really good at it and would bring "new energy." Shockingly, she told me "Whatever you need, I will help you. If you need forms, or advice…I will help you any way I can." I was shocked honestly, because I had been in such a cut throat world that helping another billing practitioner in the medical world was like helping your competition.

In short, the Reiki community believes the more people who can perform Reiki the more healing can be done, and the overall goal is to heal the planet. It's not viewed as competition, rather as an extension of ourselves. We need to honor the divine in each other. "The divine in me honors the divine in you." This truly is such a beautiful concept. This is how the world should be. Honoring each other.

My Reiki session with her was much more validating in my mind. I felt a connection with her. Maybe I was just more open to it? I had a very strong awareness of my heart beat and heart rate and felt tingling in my hands. It was like I could feel every contraction of my heart through my body, which I later realized was the energy flowing through me. This is also the feeling I get when I am giving Reiki. Sherry told me she felt a blockage in my head, like my right side was shutting off my left, and the energy flow was interrupted. "It's like there is nothing there!"

Laughing, I said, "So you're telling me my brain is empty?"

She proceeded to say she had never experienced this before, repeating, "It's like there is no energy going from the right to the left." She worked at my head for quite some time and then down my body. Stopping at my lower back and hips, she said, "You may have the feeling to pop, or push yourself, but I caution you not to do this, or you may cause more damage, allow yourself time to heal, rest, and recover."

I was completely exhausted when I left. I was instructed to drink a lot of water throughout the rest of the day. The next day, I actually felt pretty good. Sherry sent me a message the next day asking how I was and said "good luck" with my Reiki class. She also asked that I touch base when I returned to let her know how it went.

Along this journey of discovery, I am realizing that I was living in the dark. It seemed the more people I talked to, the more I realized that Reiki was pretty prevalent, and I was probably one of the few who did not know about it. I talked with my neighbor Mindy, and lo and behold she, too, trained in Reiki, she also was quit spiritual and became influential in my journey. She suggested many books along the way and my now favorite philosopher Wayne Dyer. She also introduced me to a book called *The Secret* by Rhonda Byrne and *The Shift* by Wayne Dyer, which Hope also recommended. Hope actually let me borrow the movie, which I might add was freaking awesome! These three woman became very dear friends. I really don't think they understand how influential they were to me. Wow, how could I be so blind to this whole other world? It's funny how we can put blinders on and only see what we want to. It's also funny how my eyes are wide open now, and I was seeing things very differently. It was very scary, exciting, and unbelievably overwhelming all rolled up in a neat little package.

Chapter 8
Reiki Becoming a Reality

The trip to Connecticut was very hard on me. I was in quite a bit of pain by the time we got there, but my anticipation was overshadowing the pain. The day came for my class, I was so nervous. The questions in my head:

"What if I am not any good…?"

"What if I can't learn…?"

There's so much information whirling in my head like a tornado that I was already having issues processing and remembering. I had to constantly read and re-read and still couldn't remember it all! All the information was so foreign to me. I think learning a new language would have been easier. In reality, this was a whole new language, a whole new world, and huge lifestyle change for me. Medical black and white world to a new mystical, unexplained faith-based world. At this point in the game, I felt like I was just on this conveyor belt, going along for the ride. Numb with all the new information.

The first person that I met was Steve. He was a nice "normal" enough fellow appeared to be bit younger than I was. I could sense he was nervous too, but excited. Then I met our host and instructor. Okay, so far so good. Everyone was pretty "normal" at this point. Okay, I got this! Just a normal day in the life of learning how to heal people with my hands. *Nothing weird going on here.*

Everyone arrived, and we sat in the living room that overlooked the ocean which was so peaceful and beautiful. Our instructor asked if we could all introduce ourselves, first by giving our name, where we were from, and how we became interested in Reiki. She went first. She told us her tale of being divorced, being a single mom, learning Reiki, and working at Yale. She said she felt there was more than the hustle and bustle of the everyday life. Impressive and normal! Okay, I can do this!

The second to go was a very nice woman who said she was a repeat student. She liked the class so much that she wanted to come back for a refresher. She also said it was a lot of information and felt coming back would reinforce the information. She proceeded to tell how she was a psychiatric nurse and that she also studied past lives. Huh...okay, this was getting interesting. She went on to tell us how she was able to become in tune to previous lives and actually see and feel herself in those past lives. She proceeded to tell us of her different soul experiences and what she did, man or woman, and how she died. Wow this was pretty cool. I was intrigued but was a bit weird-ed out, not gonna lie.

The next to go was the host, and she told us how she knew the instructor and how she acquired the home. Talked of her life as a massage therapist and eventually becoming a Reiki Master. Okay, pretty "normal." She explained that the home was her family home, and she used it for Reiki as it brought peace and love into the home. She also said that her dog loved to receive Reiki during classes. Oh okay, animal Reiki, I had read briefly on it, but how cool would that be! The dog was very lovey and snuggled, soaking up the love with each of us. Animal Reiki, huh, that would be pretty awesome. I love animals, and that would be a great possibility. *Okay, note to self: read more about animal Reiki.*

After this, a woman who had arrived with her daughter and son-in-law spoke. She introduced herself and began to tell us that she had many gifts. One of which was a messenger from God. I'm pretty sure I heard the song from the *Twilight Zone* play in my head! Thankfully one of her gifts was not reading minds...that I know of? I'm guessing if she could she would have called me on the carpet right then! She continued, saying she was able to get messages from God and deliver to whomever she was instructed to give them to, giving multiple examples of chance meetings in McDonald's or other places. She came from a long line of Shamans, medicine people and other spiritual healers, and this was something she had been accustomed to her whole life.

At this point, I felt kind of jealous, as I was only introduced to this fairly recently and basically lived in complete darkness for the beginning of my life. Well, it continued, she proceeded to say she could see spirits, talk to spirits. Said she enjoyed going to psychic fairs and ousting the fakes. I honestly thought this was kind of cruel but listened intently on what she was saying. I wasn't sure if I should run screaming for my life as I was going to be the sacrificial lamb…or stay? Wow…I am not in Kansas anymore Toto! I was feeling a bit uneasy to say the least.

Then it was my turn…and all I could muster to say was, "WOW! How the hell do I compete with that!?" Steve laughed along with everyone in the room and said he was thinking the same thing. I proceeded to tell my story of my patient's foot, my friend Hope, and Raphael. I figured well, hell, she's God's messenger, why can't I have Raphael at my side?

She actually said, "Yes, he is right behind you."

Oh my God…So cool! But freaking weird, and holy shit at the same time. I am not going to lie, I felt very out of place. I really questioned why I was there. Still the thoughts of getting up to "use the restroom" and just running like hell were still strong and well. But, thankfully, my husband dropped me off, and I was stuck! On a serious note, at this point in my life, the only time I would actually run is if I'm being chased by a bear, in which case I suggest you run as well!

Steve went next, and he was a very matter of fact kinda guy. Worked with computers and very "black" and "white" and factual with thoughts. He was introduced to Reiki after an illness that could never be diagnosed. After many appointments, tests, scans still no answers, he had been referred to a Reiki practitioner, and it seemed to help whereas no other treatments did. The Reiki master advised him that he should learn to do himself for continued self-help. Wow, great answer!

The next two were the daughter and son-in-law of the Messenger from God. They told their stories of how they wanted to be doctors, had natural healing in their lives already, and felt this was a natural progression. I thought this was amazing as I was finding out with my own journey that the medical world was lacking in the natural healing arts. The daughter also spoke of being an empath. I was vaguely familiar with this term and had learned that I was also an empath. I listened intently to what she was saying and found her to be very fascinating. The son-in-law told of how he could see darkness in people, stating they would have a dark cloud over them if they lied or their intentions were not good. Wow, I am learning very quickly that there is a lot of things I have NO clue about! I also was discovering a whole new world of gifted people.

The last to speak was a woman that was about to retire and wanted another type of avenue for work. Reiki had interested her, and she felt that not only would it be a great after retirement income but would also help some various health issues she had as well. Another self-helper. This was a great and very diverse group of individuals. I had no idea there were so many different types of spiritual people.

Chapter 9
Not in Kansas Anymore

After introductions, we took a break, and my head was a in a tail spin. Do I run like hell or stay? I was freaked out but at the same time so intrigued! My emotions were all over the place. I had heard the term discernment multiple times and thought, *Hmmm, wonder what that is?* Everyone but me seemed to know this term. I kept my mouth shut and figured I'd look it up. At this point, I was just trying to get through the class without bringing more attention to myself.

Our instructor turned out to be the exact person I needed to teach me. She was very factual in her education regarding Reiki, the history, how it came about, by who, when, where, why. She also works at Yale and had shared the multiple tests that had been done on people with the Reiki gift. She showed pictures of hands, one that was giving Reiki and one that wasn't.

The one that was, you could actually see the heat change and that particular machine was able to pick up energy. It was exactly what my brain needed, FACTS and evidence-based practices. My factual, literal, and skeptical medical side of my brain was appeased at this point.

The class went along with one of the books I had read on Reiki and the effects on the medical world. One story being more fascinating than the next. Steve admitted that he found the class to be what he needed as well. Factual and not voodoo-ish. This opened a discussion among the group how "everything happens for a reason" All of us having a similar tale of how we ended up in Connecticut. Canceled class, no class nearby, scheduling conflict, etc. All led us to this class with this instructor who each of us needed for one particular reason or another. The chain of coincidences for each of us was pretty spectacular.

Our first meditation and ignition was interesting. I was able to get into meditation pretty quickly and found that my voice kept repeating, "believe in yourself." It was quite obnoxious actually. I also felt that I could sense the instructor walking around the room and waving her hand doing symbols in front of us. I commented to myself, *Wow, she is really quiet!* When it was time to share, I did. My experience was pretty boring compared to others. I said I heard, "believe in yourself," over and over and over! The instructor told me that each of our experiences are what we need personally. I guess hearing that, was what I needed. I asked about discernment at this time. She explained that it was a voice, or consciousness from something more than yourself.

"How the heck do you tell if its discernment or just my own expert advice?" I asked.

Laughing, the instructor explained that if an idea just pops into my head without thinking of it, then its discernment. Oh, okay...so maybe that was my discerning message. Because not only did it just pop into my head; it was making damn sure that I was paying attention as it played like a broken record.

"BELIEVE IN YOURSELF, BELIEVE IN YOURSELF, BELIEVE IN YOURSELF...!"

The next meditation and ignition, I had the sense of the room being really cold. I wasn't cold, but the air was cold. The air was crisp like during the first snowfall. Just crisp, cool, and clean. I shared my experience and was told that this was spirits in the room. Wow, cool, okay. Again, my experience not being as grand as others who imagined Indian Chiefs visiting or crystal caves. Hmmm...cold air, okay, pretty boring but again being told that we each will have our own unique experience to help us learn the way we need to learn. I'm guessing my ancestors were coming to hang out with me. Letting me know they supported me on this adventure.

The third meditation and ignition freaked me out! We were guided along a river, into a light and up the light above. I had a vision of children playing in the clouds at God's feet. The clouds were beautiful, fluffy, white with a golden hue. I could see God's feet and lower legs but no more, as if he were sitting on his throne. I also saw the man who I helped with his legs (Arin), and the man who I helped with his foot (Neil). In my vision, we greeted each other warmly and hugged like old friends seeing each other after a long time. Neil had just passed away a few months prior and asked if I would tell his wife, "I'm fine, will you quit worrying," as he rolled his eyes. I thought, *Holy crap, I am losing it, I am imaging dead kids, and these two people who I know are dead!* I was a bit unnerved by this and chose to write it down but not share it verbally with the class.

The next section taught was about Mt. Kurama near Kyoto, Japan. Our teacher went into great depth describing the sacred mountain, the numerous steps leading up the mountain, and beautiful statues along the way. As she was teaching, she was also showing us incredible pictures of when she visited the mountain. One of the sacred sculptures was of children playing. *Umm, okay, you caught my attention.* It was a memorial to honor all the children who had died prematurely. HOLY SHIT! That was my eye opener! Wow, this is real. That was exactly the validation I needed!

We continued our learning that day, and by the end, I was completely exhausted. I honestly could not wait for a burger; I was starving! I felt horribly guilty about my desire, as everyone was vegetarian. All we ate during the day was pita chips and hummus. There was trail mix, but unfortunately, the one woman had a severe peanut allergy and requested we not open the bag. I respected her wishes and begrudgingly put them away, secretly crying for peanuts and chocolate. My husband picked me up, and we went to get a bite to eat. I excitedly told him about my day. I'm thinking he heard the *Twilight Zone* song as well but listened intently.

When we got back to the hotel, I was in significant pain. My head hurt so damn bad, and by 7:30, I had fallen asleep. I felt absolutely horrible! I really felt as if I had been run over by a truck then backed over multiple times, just to make sure I was done.

The next day was more of the same. More education and meditation. Then we got to practice what we had learned. I honestly felt very uncomfortable with the prospect of people touching me or doing "voodoo" on me. We each had to do it. We took turns with each other and different people. I felt the most when the instructor joined me, feeling a huge surge in energy. That was very cool!

My biggest ah-ha moment was when I was working with Steve. We had to practice on each other. I did Reiki on him first, and he fell fast asleep and began snoring very loudly. I tried with all my might not to laugh, looking at my instructor.

"What the hell do I do now?"

"Keep going," she instructed. Once the initial shock wore off that I had this grown man snoring like a bear in hibernation—in a room full of people no less—I felt very accomplished! It says a lot to be able to relax that much. I was pretty proud of myself.

In the snoring session, I continued Reiki, feeling drawn to his abdomen. I told him what I felt, and he said he felt the same which was validating for me. He also told me that when I raised my hands away from him, he felt more. Interesting!

When he was working on me, we were practicing distance Reiki. He sat behind the table giving Reiki to a pillow as instructed. I felt like he was squeezing my head. It was quite uncomfortable, almost to the point that I asked him to stop. I knew he was not actually touching my head, but the pain was intense. The pain started in the right side of my head with a sharp and stabbing pain, then shifted to the left side then was gone. Poof, gone! It was the most amazing feeling. Afterwards I felt very giddy and was laughing and joking, like something very negative was just released in me. At this point remembering what my previous Reiki session with Sherry had revealed, remembering her say there was the lack of energy between the right and left side of my brain, I realized that a blockage surely had been cleared. Thank God!

We then practiced directing Reiki with our eyes, and I was pretending to shoot laser beams out of my eyes to Steve, both of us cracking up. During laser beam session, one of us had to close our eyes, the other person giving had to pick a spot and concentrate their gaze in that spot. The receiver had to say where they were looking. We both got it right. I actually felt his eyes staring at my forehead and began to giggle. I thought, *Oh Lord, he's going to think I'm crazy.* I apologized to him, and he said, "I didn't even see you laugh. I actually didn't see your head at all. It was as if I looked right through your head." Again, very cool and validating.

Our last meditation, I decided to lay in a lounge chair, as I was tired at this point. I got comfortable and got into meditation. All I could do was sense my surrounding. I felt like someone was doing symbols in front of me. I could see shadows through my eyelids as if someone was moving their hands in front of me. I could also smell a soft scent of flowers. I thought to myself, *Wow the instructor is so quiet. She is moving around all of us, and I can't even hear her footsteps or breathing or anything. Damn, she's good!*

After our experience, I asked her if she got up and did symbols in front of us because she was so quiet. She said, "No, I guide you into meditation, I say the prayer and words needed, then I join the group in mediation as well. I don't leave my chair. The energy needs to come from the universe not from me, so my energy is put aside."

AGAIN, HOLY SHIT! My last validation for the day!

Our trip home was uneventful. I slept a good portion of the way. What a great experience, but wow, was I exhausted. It took quite some time to recover from the weekend's events. Although I received much validation and knowledge regarding Reiki and had a much clearer understanding of its use, I still doubted my own ability to perform as I did not have all the same gifts as the other people did.

I reached out to Sherry as well to tell her about my weekend. I told her that I was so sick after. She explained that being an empath, it was too much energy at one time. She suggested that when I decide to do the master class, I may want to say a protection prayer to help shield me from so much energy.

Chapter 10
Newfound Gifts

Hope was excited to hear how the Reiki classes went. I told her all about them, and we both giggled at the weirdness of it all. I told her I felt like I needed to tap my shoes together and say, "There's no place like home," repeatedly, but overall, it was an amazing trip. I was so glad I went. I was very nervous to try what I had learned, mainly because I was afraid to fail. Hope said she would be my guinea pig, and I could practice on her all I wanted. Even with her generosity to be an experimental subject, I felt the urgency in being able to help her. The stress was overwhelming, I practiced, and I prayed I would make a difference. She said that I did. Deep down, I continued to doubt myself, thinking she was just being nice and didn't want to make me feel bad. Later, I learned in our special friendship that she told it like it was, even if it wasn't pleasant. She was a no-holds-bar kinda girl. I admired that about her.

One day, I called Hope when I was on my way to a doctor's appointment. I knew she was having a rough time and was having a lot of pain by her voice. I asked if she was okay, and she admitted she was having a really bad morning. She asked if I could come over to do Reiki. I sadly told her I was on my way to Syracuse but could try to do distance Reiki on her if she wanted to try. She said, "Absolutely," and we both agreed on 11:50, as that gave my husband and I time to get on the highway, so I could get into a meditative state. At 11:50, I said my prayer, did my symbols as I was taught, and started my session. It was strange. I could picture being in front of God, pleading with him to take her pain away. I prayed hard, and I began to cry. When I was done, I told my husband and said, "Wow, that was intense." At this point I had no clue what Hope had experienced. We told her that we would stop by to see her after my appointment.

I was in the shock of a lifetime! We got to Hope's house, and I asked, "So, did you feel anything, did it help?"

She said, "Oh my God, it was really powerful. After I got off the phone with you, I decided to change quick and go to the bathroom. On my way back to my recliner, all of a sudden, I couldn't move, Like I was paralyzed. I seriously couldn't move. I looked at the clock, and it was 11:50 exactly. I literally had to fling myself in the chair. Then the pain hit hard, and I started to cry. But with each tear drop, the pain lessened until it was gone."

We both just looked at each other in disbelief! Again, validation.

But even with the validation, I was receiving, I continued to doubt myself, thinking that she was just being nice, or that I really was just imaging this gift. In my own reality of pain and doctor's appointments, I wanted so bad to have something positive. I just wanted light, inspiration, and a feeling of purpose. It is astounding how much fear can change your life, your perspectives, hopes, and dreams. Why do we allow fear to dictate our life so much?

Just two days ago, I was told that we don't fear failure; we fear success, talking ourselves into failing, "Who am I to be great...? Who am I to have such a gift? I'm nobody special."

Had you told me this back then, I would never have understood this statement. Now it makes perfect sense. I talked myself out of success because I was afraid.

Chapter 11
Big Dreams

My life seemed to be turning around. I had a newfound gift that I was excited about. I had many dreams of opening a huge center with all forms of disciplines. From Reiki, massage, acupuncture, nutrition, physical therapy, and occupational therapy. My name for it was the ITSA Center (it's anything, and it's possible). I was tired of the corporate world of medicine and wanted change. I wanted a more natural approach to healthcare. I read anything I could get my hands on for inspiration. I read a book by Steven Theyer called *Interview with an Angel*. I read and listened to multiple meditations with Wayne Dyer, along with many books, *The Shift*, and articles. I read books from Raven Keyes about Reiki and her experience in NYC with 9-11. I was a sponge with any and everything. But the more I read, the more I doubted myself. These were brilliant minds with brilliant talent! Wow, these people are so in tune with the world, the spirits, guides, manifestation, positive thinking. Some had other abilities that go along with the Reiki like speaking with spirits, seeing auras, crystal healing, Shamanism, holy crap the talents of these people were incredible!

I felt like if these other people could do all these cool things, why would people come to me if all I had to offer was Reiki? I can't speak to the dead, I can't see auras, or visualize chakras! Crystals to me are beautiful, but I can't feel them. Hell, I can't even remember what the chakras represent half the time. With the head injury, I am not able to process the information and remember as I once did. I struggled to just remember the symbols. My doubts are definitely my own worst enemy.

Even with the doubts, I still trudged on. I practiced on multiple people and honestly got really good results. I had done distance Reiki on my grandfather, and the next day, I called and said, "Hey, how are you doing today?"

He told me, "Wow, you know, I feel great today, I woke up had a bunch of energy and was working in the garage today."

Wow…that's awesome but still second guessed if it was just a coincidence.

The next day, I went to visit him again, and asked, "How are you doing?"

He replied, "You know, I feel the best I have felt in three years!"

Wow, that was incredible. I continued to think it was a weird coincidence. As I am writing this, I would really like to go back in time and shake the hell out of this girl…slap her even and tell her to just believe in herself! But the doubt continued.

I had gone to my aunt and uncle's house one day and was talking to our neighbor friend about Reiki. She had said that she was a Level II and had thought about getting back into it. I encouraged her to do so, as she is an awesome lady. I told her I thought she would be really great! I had told her that I was signed up for the master class in Glens Falls. I was really excited about it. My aunt had asked what Reiki was and how it worked, so I began the voodoo explanation to her. But I explained the best way I could without sounding like I was completely crazy.

"Well, I'm kinda like a cell tower. I can channel energy to people for them to use for self-healing however their body decides it needs it. Sometimes it's physical, emotional, past traumas, or even traumas or issues in our body that we are not even aware of."

I feel like people who understand, truly understand. People who don't, look at you like you have five eyes, wondering which one to look at. Like now they are hearing the theme song from *Twilight Zone*!

Nonetheless, she said to me, "You know your uncle's knee has been really hurting him and maybe you could help him."

I said I'd give it a try. I sat next to him, said my prayer, did my symbols, and proceeded with distance Reiki. I have to be honest, I did not tell him I was doing this. I was told that if the soul accepts, then the Reiki will flow; if not then it won't. I figured it would do no harm to keep to myself in case he thought I was a whack job. My aunt also felt this to be a good idea as my uncle was not quite as open to this "type of stuff." That night, I asked my aunt how his knee was, and she said it was much better. The next morning, she said the pain was completely gone.

Wow. Giggling, I told my aunt, "Okay, now you can tell him."

She did and he thanked me and told me, "My pain's gone, it feels great!"

Umm, so chalk it up to another coincidence or realize I have a gift.

I have had many stories like the above but continued to second guess my abilities. I had been to multiple Reiki practitioners in the area, and I myself did not get great results with the pain management. I felt very pulled to this but continued to wonder if it was real. I wanted so much to be this amazing Reiki master that people from states away knew. You'd hear my name and say, "Wow, I know her. She's incredible!"

You see, this was my downfall. I was under the assumption that my ability was going to be measured by my popularity or how big my Reiki center was. I was missing the entire picture completely. All I needed to do was believe in myself. That I—just me—was enough! In time, I would have an epiphany.

Chapter 12
Reiki Master Acheived

The time came to go to my master class in Glens Falls, NY. I took Sherry's advice and prayed for protection. What a great experience! The people I met were absolutely wonderful. I, however, again felt very out of place because many of them had been practicing for years. About half already had their master level and were upgrading to the Holy Fire, and as with all the other Reiki masters had multiple other talents to offer. Umm, yeah, I was first introduced to this whole new world less than a year ago, and I was only a Reiki Level II for six months. I was such a newbie and completely in the dark on a lot of the information to this world.

The woman next to me was such a beautiful soul. So sweet and understanding in every way. Her presence made me at peace. She was exactly the person I needed to sit next to. Her name was Valerie. She had been practicing for many years, also was very in tune to crystal healing. To me, I thought crystals were beautiful rocks. I didn't get a particular feeling or vibe from them.

"They're just rocks," but she explained that she could indeed feel their energy. Some had very good energy, made her feel a certain way, and others had bad energy. I have heard people say, "Oh, wow, this one is really snarky," or "This one is not a good one for me." Here I was like, "Oh, they are so pretty." I was very fascinated and honestly envious that so many others had these other amazing traits. Again, being introduced to so many other aspects of spirituality and healing.

Another woman, Jasmin, was able to clear past Karmic events, traumatic soul splitting (I can't remember the actual term for it), but basically traumatic events can split the soul from the body, and it needs to be healed. Wow, okay, I was truly interested in what she was telling us. She was a very fascinating woman. A very energetic and sparkly woman. People were drawn to her. But to listen to her, you'd think she was God herself. Her abilities were incredible. She gave us a display of her ability with Valerie saying when she was born that there was a traumatic event during her birth. Val listened with wide eyes, and Jasmin's necklace started to circle, and she chanted some things and explained what she was doing. Her necklace was spinning wildly and then stopped. Val then said that, yes, she almost died when her mom gave birth to her. Jasmin then looked at me, showed me her phone, and it said 7:17 and asked me when my accident was. I told her that it was 7/18. She told me that the universe had decided that I was supposed to die in that accident. That I was very lucky, and I should take it as a near-death experience. I was honestly pretty shocked. I knew I was lucky, but to hear someone say that I was supposes to die was like knocking the wind right out of me. Now I felt even more pressure to be great. I thought that if God had spared me, then I am meant to do great things. Honestly this was extremely overwhelming. I couldn't remember what I had for breakfast. How the hell was I going to run these centers and be the best of the best?

The meditations again brought about validation not only for me but for Valerie. It was strange as with such a big group all of our experiences had some sort of similarity to it. Either a word spoken, music, darkness, silence. When we shared, it was like people were like, "Oh, I had that, too," which to me was a validation because how do you get all these people in the same room and not speak a word to each other, but still see or hear similar things? It was incredible.

When it came time to practice, I practiced with Valerie and three other ladies. The one lady, Melanie, I remember because after our practice time, she had a message for each of us that we needed to hear. My message was that I get my energy from the sun and that I should be in nature more, especially in the sun. It was so funny that she said that because at break just prior, I had taken my shoes off to walk in the grass. I raised my face to the sun to feel the warmth. I was so overwhelmed with all that took place in class and the night prior being told I should have died. I just had to walk in the grass to regroup and bring my peace back. What she said made complete sense to me. I love nature. There is nothing more relaxing than being in nature for me.

During our practice time, Val was our "victim," and for whatever reason, I went to her left shoulder as others took places at her head, feet, and stomach. We provided Reiki to her and then shared our experience after. Val told me that, "I'm not sure why you went to my shoulder, but I didn't even know it was hurting until you went to that side. I must have strained it when I was walking my dog." It wasn't like I thought, *Oh I need to go to her left shoulder...* I just did. Later in class, we were talking about intuition and the importance of being in tune to it and how it can be used to provide Reiki. Recognizing the energy in people and especially when it is "off," I mentioned to Val, "Man, I wish I was good at that."

She just looked at me and said, "Are you freaking kidding me? You went right to my arm. That's a gift."

I explained that I really didn't know what my gifts were, so we got into an in-depth conversation about different gifts. I told her that I was able to read people well. But just figured I was observant. She laughed and said she was asked to tell how someone was feeling by looking at a picture. She got every single one right. She said this may be my gift as well. I didn't realize it was a gift.

I told her, "I thought it was just paying attention to people."

She laughed again and said, "Jess, not everyone can do that, that is your gift."

Huh, I thought, *Well, hell, I can do that! Sweet, I will take it as a gift because that comes easy to me.* I thought somehow it was cheating to pay attention to a way a person walks, talks, their facial expressions, physical movements, or the all-out tale tell their eyes. Eyes are very telling. But hey, you say it's a gift, I will accept it. Yeah, I'm gifted! I earned my Master Level Reiki in Holy Fire and felt very proud of my accomplishment. My kids lovingly called me "Mama Yoda."

Chapter 13
Geographic Fix Fails

In July, my family and I went on our dream vacation. In my mind, this trip was the fix all! I had high hopes it was going to be this huge spiritual awakening, seeing the majestic mountains and beautiful countryside. It was going to take my depression away and "show me the light." I thought if I could just get away from it all, it would go away! I would wake up from this and live my life like I did before the accident.

It was the most wonderful, beautiful, and amazing experience. However, was not the cure all I had hoped it to be. We drove across the country and saw national and state parks along the way. We stayed in Ohio at Port Clinton, went to Put n Bay Island. This was the first time my kids had taken a ferry ride. It started out pretty good. We then continued west, stopping at different areas, making our way to Sioux Falls, South Dakota. Holy cow, this is by far my favorite city I have been to yet. That is saying a lot because, deep down, I am a country girl through and through. This city was clean, the people were nice, bike trails along the city and parks that were easy access and easy to ride. The city was built near a water fall park. The coolest part to me was the statues all over the city. Every year, hundreds of artists submit a statue to the city and all the people that come vote on the one they like best. At the end of the year, the winning statue is purchased by the city and becomes a permanent fixture to the city. Oh my God, there were so many beautiful statues everywhere! One of my favorites was an incredible bronze angel. She was sitting with her legs bent with her arms hugging her legs. Head resting on her knees, tilted to the side. Her wings were relaxed behind her. It was breathtaking. I loved the feel of this place. I would definitely visit again! Even as I write about it, it brings back such a warm feeling.

We continued to Rapid City and Custer National Park. We saw Mount Rushmore, Iron Highway, Needles Highway, the Bad Lands, Devils Tower, Sturgis, Wall Drug, Mount Rushmore Cave and Adventure Center, Hot Springs, an Archaeological site for the world's largest mammoth dig, Lady Dignity, and the movie site for *Dances with Wolves*. It was awesome.

We then continued west into Wyoming, holy cow…flat nothingness for miles and miles. We went to Casper, and there pretty much was nothing but prairie land for hundreds of miles until we got to Casper. There was one town that had population of under 100 people in it. Thank God for this little town, as we were running on fumes, and this was the only gas station for miles! Casper, however, was much larger and was a pretty city just in the middle of nowhere. Casper had a beautiful mountain back drop with one of the prettiest sunsets I had seen thus far. The sky was a vibrant orange! We decided to treat ourselves to a nice restaurant, and it was suggested to go the Fire Rock Steakhouse. Wow, it did not disappoint; let me tell you, it was delicious! When we first arrived, my husband went to the bar to get a drink. While there, he met a lovely couple. They chit-chatted back and forth, and the man asked where we were going. By this time, I had arrived and joined in the conversation. We told him we were on our way to the Grand Tetons and then Yellowstone.

"Oh my brother in law works in Yellowstone Lodge, tell him I said hi!"

Oh, wow, okay, we will. Such nice people out west!

Onto the Grand Tetons we went. I cannot even begin to express how beautiful they were. There seriously is no written word that could give it any justice. I have never seen such beautiful mountains in my life. The scenery was like I had seen in books but way better. I could breathe the air and feel the breeze and sun on my face. It was rejuvenating to say the least. I have to say this was worth every ounce of flat land I had seen for the hours prior to these magnificent views. We saw bison by the hundreds roaming free. As we were driving, we saw a line of cars on the side of the road. We asked a passerby what was going on and were told, "It's a moose!"

The motorist was incorrect; it wasn't a moose. It was the granddaddy of bull elks walking only feet from us! He was a stunning creature with huge antlers. I was in awe that he was only feet from us. He didn't seem to be bothered that we were all just watching him and taking pictures, and he calmly ate his dinner. We also saw our first cow moose, and she was majestic! I always felt that the moose was my spirit animal. I had been drawn to them for years now. In fact, a majority of our honeymoon was spent driving hours to spot a moose in Maine, but we never saw one. It took driving to Wyoming to see our very first moose! I was ecstatic. Not only did we see her, but her baby as well. I seriously wanted to cry. She was so beautiful!

Next was Yellowstone, and it was very beautiful. The geysers were cool to see, boiling water just coming out of the earth was definitely a site to see. Man, do they smell like rotten eggs though—peeuuu! And yes, we saw Old Faithful erupt and found the man's brother in law to say hi. What an amazing artist and such a cool guy. We talked with him for at least an hour.

"Let me guess, you were at the Fire Rock," he said.

Laughing, we said, "Why yes, yes we were"

He was such a fascinating guy to talk with. He told us a lot about the wildlife in the area as well as the history. Yellowstone in all its glory was unfortunately also the first area where I had an extreme panic attack. There were so many people around; the traffic was insane. At certain parts, the roads were narrow and extremely dangerous. At one point, a panic attack hit strong. I started to sweat, felt nauseous, and was death gripping the sides of the seat and door. My kids and husband were laughing, saying, "Oh, it's fine, Mom, its nothing!" but to me I had this sudden urge to get the fuck out of that car…get me out now! I really thought I was going to die. That horrible moment passed. The next day, we heard of a nine-year-old girl being gored by a bison. So sad, our hearts went out to her. Fortunately, she survived.

Next stop was my all-time dream, Montana. I have dreamed of seeing Montana for years. I never thought it would happen. As we crossed the Montana line, we whooped and hollered for joy. We stopped in Butte, Kalispell, Whitefish, Columbia Falls, Flat Head Lake, and spent a majority of our time on Lake Five, just on the outskirts of Glazier National Park. I thought Grand Tetons was impressive. Holy shit! Seriously, Glacier National was beyond words. We were able to see stunning landscapes that could have ended up in the National Geographic. Then it happened…not only in one day did we see a bear, but we saw a Momma moose, her baby, another female walk just feet from us to the lake we were headed to, but we saw a bull moose. He was absolutely gorgeous. We watched him for some time eating in the lake. He then crossed our path just in front of us. I was so excited but terrified at the same time. He was huge, and I knew he could seriously injure any one of us if he felt we were a threat. We just stood as still as we could and watched as he crossed our path and continued to walk on his way. This was a dream come true. On our way back to the campground, the sickening feeling struck me again as we were going through the mountain pass. I felt the panic set in again as we were driving on the roads with the cliffs and treacherous curves. I again felt like I was going to die. I could not go on that road again. My panic was too great. I was terrified! Later, we found out that in that same area, a family had a boulder fall on their car, killing a 14-year-old girl. I can tell you that I thought it weird that I had two panic attacks and after found that people had been injured. I was hoping this was a coincidence, as the panic attacks were horrible. If I was going to sense danger, I'd prefer in it a form of a neon sign or something instead of a panic attack!

    Besides the panic issues that I had, I felt so alive when I was in Montana. I felt free and just alive. I don't really know any other way to describe it. I didn't want to leave. My heart sank as we crossed back over the state line into North Dakota, as I knew the trip was coming to an end. I would have to return to the real world soon.

    On our way home, we stopped at multiple landmarks including a pictograph cave and Custer's Last Stand and the Battle of Little Big Horn. It was surreal to think that this battle took place right where we stood. I couldn't help to feel angry at the humans for being so greedy. I just couldn't understand why people fought to take away from one another, and I was quickly reminded that even today, we all fight among each other. Sadness crept over me as I mourned for people I had never met. Families that were torn apart. Graves that were still present. This lingering sadness accompanied me for quite some time, even after we left.

We continued on our way, passing thousands of acres of sunflowers and hay bales along with wheat fields. For as far as you could see in any direction, it was one crop or another. It was amazing to see. Just incredible to think about the time and effort it takes to plant and yield these crops. It really makes you appreciate our farmers.

We continued to Duluth, Minnesota. I have to tell you that Minnesota was never really on my bucket list, but it was absolutely beautiful. The city is right on Lake Superior, which is an enormous lake. Had you not known it was a lake, you would have thought you reached the ocean. There were jagged rocky shores, beaches, ships, ship yards, board walks, cool little shops and old-fashioned restaurants that have been around for over 100 years. I really enjoyed walking along the rocks, looking at light houses and skipping rocks. The weather could not have been more perfect. There was one shore that had black sand that was from the iron deposits. The kids at this point had enough of the camper and travel life with Mom and Dad and asked to go home. Again, my heart sank to know my adventure was soon over. two days, later we were home.

Chapter 14
Home to Reality

Back home to reality. Back home to doctor appointments and therapy. The depression was quickly setting in. I had lost hope of doing Reiki or anything other than appointments. My dream of Montana came and went. I was thankful for my beautiful memories but didn't want just memories, I wanted my freedom back. Reality was that the trip took a lot out of me. I enjoyed everything with a price. The price was pain and realizations of my limitations. The next few months were very dark for me. The pain levels were high and poorly controlled. The injections into my body were horrible and didn't work. My brain function seemed to be getting worse. I found myself in spirals of darkness. I tried to pull myself out, but it became too unbearable and more and more difficult to do. Often times, I found myself wondering why the hell I lived if I wasn't going to be able to do what I wanted all the time. Up until this point in my life, I had witnessed depression but could not fully understand it. Now I did, all too well. I also could understand why people took their own lives. As said before, suicide was becoming more tantalizing and unfortunately understandable.

December, I had to undergo testing for my cognitive abilities. This was a major trigger for pain, migraines, as well as the very real punch in the face that there were more cognitive issues than I realized. This sent me into a huge tailspin. I realized that I was not going to be able to practice nursing safely anymore. There was no way I was risking killing someone because I couldn't think "right." I found myself sobbing uncontrollably in my doctor's office, begging for some sort of relief.

She started me on antidepressants, sleeping pills, and instructed me to take the pain medication that I had been fighting all along. I felt like a failure. It's not easy being the caregiver all your life to having to ask for help. I thought I had my life figured out. Then when it changed, I thought I had a new plan. That new plan turned into an overwhelming roller coaster.

The medication caused major nightmares. I wasn't sure which med caused them but was not impressed. I stopped all but the antidepressant. I lost 10 pounds in two weeks, which to me seemed a benefit versus a side effect. I guess that is perspective. The nightmares turned into weird but tolerable dreams. I still was not sleeping, and the pain at night kept me awake, so I attempted to take the pain meds again, causing nightmares. I tried a half-tablet, and this seemed to help. Okay, so the pain was now tolerable, but I was still not sleeping. I was continually waking up between 2:00 to 4:00 AM every stinking morning. This was getting old. One night, I tried to take the sleeping pill. A few minutes later, I went into the kitchen and had nearly blacked out. My hands began to shake, I was instantly weak, my knees shook. I had waves of nausea and felt as if I was going to pass out at any moment. My daughter had to help me back to bed. Nope…not taking that again!

The anger quickly reared its ugly head. My anger was horrible. I was mad at the world, my husband, my kids, myself, and especially the other driver. I realized that I never dealt with the loss. I never really dealt with the other driver. I was trying to bypass the grief. But the grief hit and hit hard and swift! Something needed to change and change fast, or I was going to lose this battle.

At four weeks after starting my antidepressant, I felt that the tornado from hell that I was in was at least stopped. I still, however, was not where I wanted to be. I was still not on a good sleep schedule. At six weeks is when I felt the cloud start to lift. I was able to stand, finally seeing some sunshine. I could see light.

Chapter 15
Something Finally Clicked

Something in me clicked. I felt the urge to journal again as well as meditate. One morning at the 2:00 waking hour, I decided to get up and journal. It was a trick I had learned in this crazy past year but shoved aside because quite frankly was sick and damn tired of writing all of it down. It was 2:50 AM, I grabbed my journal and set out to the living room. My mind was a whirlwind. "What do I write?" turned to writing for an hour. In this hour, I had finally realized that I am enough. I can help people just by being me. I didn't need special powers or psychic abilities to be good at Reiki. I can be the light for other people just by being me. I typically would say hi to people, purposely making eye contact with them. I purposely would ask people how they were and call them out if I thought they weren't okay just so they had someone to talk to and knew that someone cared enough to "see." My realizations were pouring onto the page. I felt lifted, relieved, and rejuvenated. I felt my purpose! My real purpose for the first time. Not only did I feel it, I knew it.

My purpose may not be the big medical center with natural healing. I may not be the greatest known or even a well-known Reiki master. Hell, people may not even remember my name. But I know that every person I meet, I can make a difference. Even if it's just a smile, a nice gesture, teach what I remember, and to just love as hard as I can. My purpose is to just be me, the real me. Not allowing the bad events in my life to dictate the me I needed to be. I am enough. In this journal, I also got the phrase "Be the Light" and a picture came to my mind, that if I'm the light for one person, then that person is light for another, and so on. I have the potential of helping a lot of people, just by being me.

I also had to come to terms with my fear, depression, and their debilitating effects on not only the mind but also the physical body. Until you are in this position, it is not something you realize. How could you? Unless you personally go through this, you could NOT possibly understand. I wish more healthcare workers understood this instead of saying, "I understand," when they literally have no fucking clue!

The debilitating effects of pain, depression, and lack of sleep is a horrible cycle. They all feed off each other like parasites! The cycle is real. It's scary, especially when you try to tell yourself you have it under control. Then in the blink of an eye, your thoughts go to the barrel of a gun.

Chapter 16
New Perspectives

Manifestation is something I had read about, even tried to dabble in. I had spoken to my neighbor, and she told me that when you send out confusing messages to the universe, then you will not be able to manifest what you really want. You need to be clear on what it is that you want. Makes sense, or so I thought. I wanted to be healed but was afraid of failing. Well, what message is that? Did I want to heal or fail? I wanted money, but was afraid I wasn't going to make enough money to support my family. So, what was that message? Did I want money or was I afraid of it? I wanted to be a great Reiki Master but didn't have enough confidence in my ability. Okay, so again, what message was that? Did I want to do it or not? No wonder I had so much trauma and "what the hell" moments. I was the walking contraction in my own life story.

As time is passing, I am having more ah-ha moments and clarity in my own life. Like I need to quit contradicting myself. No wonder the universe is confused! Hell, no wonder I was confused. I need to own my fear and depression. I need to own it like it's my bitch. It will not control me anymore! I need to own money. There is plenty in the world for me; it is not scarce, it is not evil, it is a tool to help others, and it will be my bitch. I need to own that I am really talented, and I have the ability to help people, even if it's just being present and being me. I have a gift; in fact, I have many gifts. My gifts are going to be my bitch...I own them!

Attitude and positive thinking are truly skills. Owning your actions is also an important skill. In life, it's a lot easier to blame others for your issues or failures in life. What we all need to realize is that life is free will. Freedom to choose what, when, how, if, or where we live. Freedom may not come in the form of control over others, but it does come in the form of control of how we react to others. I am not going to give that power to anyone else again. I am going to own my happiness. I'm taking responsibility for my poor choices and choosing to learn from them. I am going to own my love, my peace, and my freedom to be me.

God may have knocked me on my ass, multiple times. But it's because I wasn't listening. I choose to learn from this. I choose to be a healer, a wounded healer. I choose light!

Chapter 17
Realizations and Validation

I started to do Reiki again! The other day, I did Reiki on a 91-year-old man who was in a coma from sepsis then a stroke. Him and his family are very dear to me.

I prayed as usual, did my symbols, and just loved as hard as I could. Putting my ego aside, I set my intention for him to use the love and energy I was channeling as he needed. Either to pass peacefully or come back to some quality of life, whatever he chose. The next day, I received word that he was awake, eating, drinking and talking. What a miracle! I would like to believe I had something to do with it. I will take it as a win, as his family had more time with him, and no matter the reason that is good enough for me. His family had a few more days of telling each other they loved one another before he did finally pass peacefully. His wife and family had said multiple times they were so grateful that I was there. This in my mind was worth it. I was the light for the family in a time when they needed it. This I can do; I am no longer overwhelmed thinking I have to play God, or have all these supernatural gifts to know I make a difference in people's lives. I just need to be present. How simple, I can do that!

Throughout the entire process of learning in this past year, its been reinforced that hindsight is 20/20. I look back and even as I write this, I can see so many things that happened and can now understand why. Wouldn't it have been much easier had I just realized back then that I was enough? I would have not gone through so much pain and suffering. With that though, I have become a wounded healer. Now that I am a wounded healer, I will have a greater understanding of suffering. My hopes are that people will be able to relate to me because I'm just like them. A normal, non-supernatural, spiritual, loving, caring individual who's just a simple country girl at heart. I'm just me!

Chapter 18
Making a Difference

One of my recent days while scrolling on social media, I noticed a story about a young man who caught my eye. He told of a story when he was young how he went from foster home to foster home. Each home proclaiming to be his new mom and dad. Each home at one point or another discarded him. The everlasting feeling of abandonment led to anger. The anger led to behavioral issues. Each home rotated quicker than the previous. His last home, he said, was different, very different. He figured if they were going to get rid of him, let's get it over with. His behavioral issues became significant. No change in his foster parents; they were still there. Three years went by, and he thought, "I better step up my game, they are going to get rid of me anyway," so he started to steal and get in trouble with the law. This landed him in jail. He got one phone call, and it was to his foster father.

"I got arrested and I am in jail. Can you bail me out?"

His foster father responded, "yes, but not tonight. I will see you tomorrow," and as promised, the next day, he bailed the boy out. He told the young man that, "You see you can keep doing what you are doing, that is your choice if you want to continue this path. But you need to understand that we don't think you are a problem. We love you no matter what."

How powerful this was to a young man who thought he was just a menace to society, "so why bother?" He went on to say that had his foster father not shown him that unconditional love, he would have ended up in jail permanently, on drugs, or even dead. His new life mission was to help others understand that helping just one person, taking that time with just one person can make a difference. Helping a child in need, an elderly person with no family or friends as all of them have passed before them, a neighbor or even just a smile to the clerk at the grocery store.

Everyone has struggles that they are dealing with, and none of us wear a sign that says, "Hi, my name is ____ and I am dealing with ____."

Robin Williams is a perfect example. The king of comedy. To the public, he was so happy, always smiling, laughing. Bringing joy to so many. Secretly, he was battling depression to the depths of his soul. In great sorrow, we lost an amazing man and the world was shook.

"He always looked so happy…" How many times do we hear this after someone commits suicide? More often than not.

The grocery clerk that is grumpy and appears to hate her job may have just had her electric shut off because her husband was killed in battle and is just trying to stay afloat. The person behind you driving erratically blinking their lights at you, might be on the way to the hospital to witness his wife's possible death as she is having emergency surgery. The little boy who is the bully in school may be being beaten at home and is hiding his bruises and doesn't know how to deal with his anger. The woman at the grocery store who accidentally bumped her cart into you, maybe she's trying to hold it together for her kids because she just found out that her husband has been unfaithful. The man that is at the gas station who is too preoccupied to notice that he just cut you off in line, maybe he just left the hospital where his child died. The teenage girl who is a "slut," maybe she had been raped since the age of four, and that's what she was told love was. If we all just took one person to be the light for, just one. Think how different that person's life would or could be. All we need to do is care enough not to assume. All we need to do is care enough to notice. Sometimes, all we need to do is say, "Hi, how are you today?" and actually LISTEN to the response! If they say, "okay," or, "I'm fine," it's okay to say, "That was not convincing," and then say, "I just want you to know that I care. I hope you have a great rest of your day," giving them the most heartfelt smile you can. That act alone could make the difference if someone decides to go home and end their life or not.

We all go through tough times in our lives. Some greater than others. I hope if nothing else, my book can be an inspiration to just be you. Don't change you because of bad events. Cut yourself some damn slack! We all need to quit comparing ourselves to the next person and just be the best us we can be. God knows we are imperfect; hell, he created us. Had I kept comparing myself, I wouldn't have written this book. Like, seriously, who the hell am I to write a book? I'm a nurse, a mom, a wife, a Nama Duck—I'm not a famous author or philosopher. I don't have a Master's Degree or Ph.D., and I'm not well-versed in the supernatural. Who am I to write a book…?

I'm me!

And I'm hoping that "just me" can help "just you" be the best amazing you that you can be.

I have preached to many young people that, "You need to love yourself fully and first, so you can be the best version of yourself for others." I was told that sounded selfish, and I said, "No, it's necessary." This is something I, too, had to learn.

Wouldn't the world be a nicer place if we just cut ourselves and others a little slack? We don't need to be grand, or rich, or thin, or perfectly beautiful. We just need to love ourselves for who we are.

When we truly love ourselves, I believe that we become at peace with ourselves. When we are peace, then the people around us get the benefit as well. They have more peace, then that spreads.

In my last journal entry, I wrote "Be the Light." My vision for the statement is me being as bright as I can, that light shines on to the people around me, then they become brighter, then their light shines to the people around them and so on. If I love myself for me, I become peace, I become the light for others. THAT is my purpose. How simple…love myself. In my journal, I drew the image I saw. A stick figure with abundance of love, happiness, money, and light!

Be the Light

"I want to be the light for others, so they can be the light for others, and so on."
- BY JESSICA MARICLE

A book about inspiration and spiritual growth, a woman tells her tale with intention of helping others with her recovery from a car accident, loss of income, career, and the ideals that she had everything figured out.

She shares her battle with depression, anxiety, PTSD, and suicidal thoughts. In her journey she not only discovers herself, but her purpose and gifts in life as well.

Reading many books along the way did, in fact, help her, but also left her feeling at times that her simple life was no match for the world of authors, supernatural gifts, Ph. Ds, Masters degrees, or philosophers. She was just her… which she discovered was all she needed to be.

It is easy to tell someone to "get over it," or "you need to be positive." How do you do that if you don't have any clue how to even take the first step? Her intention is that this book will inspire someone to take that first step. Her beautiful friend Hope said it best when she said, "God knows I am a screw up, and he still loves me anyway," as she would beam ear to ear with a huge, glistening smile.

Every event in our life can be looked at in a positive way or negative way. It's our choice which way we are going to look at it. But from the depths of hell, it's difficult to see any positive other than, "Well, at least it's warm!" But even in the depths of hell, there is still hope. There is still love and light. We just need to be brave enough to look and ask for help. Realizing this does not make us weak. It makes us human.

Author Contact Information:

mariclesreiki1122@yahoo.com